Lost Verses & Found Souls

A Collection of Poems

Dr. Nisha Jha

BookLeaf Publishing

India | USA | UK

Made with ❤ on the BookLeaf Publishing Platform

www.bookleafpub.in

www.bookleafpub.com

Dedication

To my dear husband, family, and friends.....

Preface

*I am aware that introverted people like myself have never
had easy letting go. The daily emotional rollercoaster and
beating that one's body and heart must endure wears on
one's head. As a result, especially throughout my higher
education, I began writing as a way to escape from my
everyday life.*

*At times, the only thing that kept me sound and sane
without feeling overburdened was my writing.*

*I continued to write about all of my feelings, experiences,
uncertainties, worries, joys, and curiosity, including self-
discovery, love, passion, science fiction, mythology, the
medieval ages, doubts, rage, anxiety, and perseverance.*

*I found solace in writing poems without ever weighing on
the expertise of vocabulary that I usually see bestowed by
renowned poets. I never once imagined that my journey
would be engraved in the form of a book.*

*The book Lost Verses & Found Souls is not just a poetry
book, but it is about my passion for words and how it
restructured my life through all the anguish and
uncertainties.*

*I hope that this book reaches and encourages everyone who
desires to write but envisages their writing as not polished
enough:*

"Write if it feels right, don't stop the words from flowing, and don't overthink that it's not worthy."

If it's the only thing that makes sense, then that's the only thing that counts.

Finally, I want to convey that achieving this milestone has only been possible because of the love and support offered by my family and friends.

Acknowledgements

First and foremost, I am incredibly grateful to my wonderful husband, Apoorv, for always believing in me, encouraging me to publish, and helping me with everything, from proofreading to offering feedback. This dream of publishing came true only because of his unwavering love and faith.

I want to express my deepest appreciation to my amazing parents, in-laws, and other family members for always believing in my writing, even when I was irresolute.

I would especially like to thank Bookleaf Publishing for providing me with the platform to express my words and bring this dream to life.
Lastly, I would like to express my heartfelt gratitude to my friends—for believing in me, supporting me, and always being there to share in my victories and offer consolation during trying times.

This book is a testament to their belief in me, for which I will always be thankful.

1. Red Heart

I revolved around the globe
In the search for hope,
A lasting miracle
That lost all the scope.

A battle of ego
Of transitioning anger,
Heart full of pain
Mind full of danger.

A thought so broad
Like the vastness of a forest
A brain filled with chaos
Like the lost sunsets.

But the red remained.
Beating and ingrained
Shrouded in the misery of agonizing grains
Of past memories and buried rains.

2. The Lost Rains

The kitchen floor is littered with dust
The ceiling fan is full of iron rust,
The room is quiet and sound
No one is near to hear around,
It's been ages since anyone came here
The home of love has become the house of despair,
No signs of children laughing and playing with pens,
It all stopped, I don't know when
Now, all that is left is the past remains
The buried memories and the lost rains.

3. Agony

In the eerie silence of rain that patters
There once was a time filled with laughter,
Of whispered love and heartfelt promises
Of taken oaths and stolen kisses,
And now I sit alone in the dark
As the path of tears on my face spark,
The pain and agony is too much to bear
I wish for the calm that won't come near,
It's been years since she's been gone
And I've tried to live all alone,
As will come short day by day,
Now, death seems only a breath away.

4. Firefly

She was the firefly in my darkest night
Always looming with flecks of light
Providing a path to my sailed ship,
I watch her enthralled
Buzzing with energy
Carrying the power of light,
She is resplendent
And so fragile to touch,
But I didn't give in to my desire to cage her
To make her mine forever,
Though I am a moth to her flame
You can't trap something innocent
And watch it drain away,
So I just sit and watch her in vain
Soaking her tranquility in sacred rains

5. Wheelbarrow

Chasing you around, I walk the circles of my town,
I jog miles for your signs, creating a meadow
Of my memories mixed with your shadow,
But you vanished
All dreams and hopes tarnished,
I used to play guitar strings
Now, it's just my heart's beating that is creating a
rhythm
Of your melancholic melodies
Indicating reducing breaths like ticking off time,
So, I take turns visiting your last residing
Hopping on a wheelbarrow towards the grave of your
shrine.

6. Ruins

A mile-long road awaits in front of me
To take me to the place that haunts my dream
It was a sanctuary of love and what used to be,
Now, stand in the ruins, a beautiful house
Of wrecked fences and walls worn-out
All warmth is lost from hardwood floors
The roof that leaks, and the creaking of doors,
But it saw once the curves of life
The colorful days and soulful nights.

7. Rain Again

When it rains again,
I will adore you with eyes full of pain.
When it rains again,
I will forgrant your every wish insane.
When it rains again,
We will dance together hands clasped again.
When it rains again,
I will write you songs of cuckoo in the rains.
When it rains again,
We will drink coffee too hot in vain.
When it rains again,
I will buy you a dress with a long train.
When it rains again,
I will pepper sweet kisses on your curves and plains.
When it rains again,
I promise I will never leave again.

8. Take Me Home Today

Erase my sorrows and burden
Hold my hands in thunder,
Those entwined fingerlocks
Keep in place when death knocks,
I am bleeding and bruised
Battered in red hues,
Waiting for you to this day
I hope you take me home today.

A forlorn desire,
A craving so grey
I wanted to be a siren of worldly prey,
Touches away I wanted to keep
The wound was there but never too deep,
I paid a price for my whimsical wants
Awaiting the return of the forgotten path,
With a passing goodbye
And a whisper of a kiss

Lost in the shadows of my materialistic greed
Now I am ashes of black in fairy sheets,
A silent cry
A broken plea
To someone I love
And someone I need
Waiting for him to this day
I hope you take me home today.

9. She

She is boiled up and burned down
Exhausted with the same frowns
Upon a face, Oh, so lovely,
Where did the smile vanish?
The dread settled on the flawless beams
Could not touch
Even the peeking streams,
As she lies motionless
On the grassy hay
So quiet and sound
Civilizations away
A full of life and zest
The lady had come with a colorful fest,
But she never moved
The wind touched
The birds crooned
The rain splashed
Then autumn swooned
Then, one bleary winter
She got up and rose

With misery and agony seeping into bones
Faltering every step that she took
Ribs broke with the breath she pushed
The mind of mess, and the life full of chaos
Mahogany-like hair shaped like halos,
She reminisces about the unfathomable deeds
She saw him dead, so death she needs
Her brain won't shut the overdrives
Now the pain is all on she thrives
Devil, take a pity, she asks in prays
Staring round the clock at bleary grays
Then, one fine morning, she left the town
She hitchhiked to the devil's ground
With soul on platter and touch of blood
She submitted the deity till every drop.

10. Albatross

He was an injured hummingbird,
Tossed carelessly at the orifice of my window
Whimpering, his heart beating a mile
As I try to soothe the pain
Embraced in the cradle of my arms
I lull him to sleep with my rhymes.

11. Repentance

She is free now,
Since you have let her go
She breathes a little easily
And lives a little more
Her world revolves around her now
Not you anymore,
You did hurt her
You did cause her agony
But when you ask her to forgive you
It's something in vain.
She is confused as hell
For what is there to forgive
She does not understand
It's not in her hands to forgive you,
What you did was cruel
How you tormented her to satiate your ego
Just to deal with her moving on from you without any
revenge
How selfish you became by showing off,
But at last, you repent,

You repent for something to someone that is not theirs to
give
You let her go
Now, only do you realize how precious was she?
Maybe, and maybe not
And you are obtuse now
Not knowing what to do
How to deal with guilt, which you never had to
So you survive, searching for salvation
And then you stand in front of your reflection
Asking penance for your pinnacled sins
And what you get is your inner self pointing at you
That it has always been only you who can forgive
yourself,
But it's incomprehensible to you
You are baffled and shattered by this agonizing
responsibility
So you barely whisper a broken 'No' to your mirage
And start searching nooks for atonement.

12. Tale Of A Broken Girl

I want to shout
To make everybody hear,
The silent trauma and quiet battles
And the inferno that rages,
I want to let it flow like a volcano about to blow.

I am burdened and ghosted by the past memories,
How to undress these insecurities?
Why the malevolence at the innocence's cost,
Is the price of our love betrayal at your worst?

Alas! This pain does not leave.
Only she can subdue this grief.
She knows this, but still, she wants this.
She doesn't know how to reach
To the heights of freedom again,
Where the wings unwrap to release the insecurities
trapped.

All say don't expect but how to stop this prospect,
The chain of doubts, the creeping burn
Of jealous heart and the mind of urns,
Waking up at night in cold sweats
Holding the sheet when desperate,
Will anyone even understand?
If I tell the tale of a broken girl
Lively once and now a shrine of hurt.

The overwhelming urge to hold someone
Onto the palms of your whole sun
To not scare them away
But even then, they should want to stay
Because she is worth the trouble
And they are willing to play this rubble.

But when the broken girl again tries
She gets the guys that don't play fair
They are independent and aware
They favor non-attachments and chasing games
In case when they meet someone better than her,
So, they keep their distance,
She never gets a guy who can affirm the ties
Of connecting hearts, comprehending her past
And supports the worst with no judgment reserved.

The broken girl has understood
That it might take her blood
To toughen up the scenes and remain unseen,
This world is not for her
She is, after all, a falling fern,
Of autumn's gone by
So she has stopped tries
Of finding someone conscientious.

Maybe time has moods, and it will swing
Bring happiness in her life again
Till then, she will heal and make herself feel,
All safe, sound, cherished, and ground,
To the self-love journey of falling deeper,
And those who lost her will always mourn,
After all, they lost a keeper.

13. Burden

If I am a burden
Then leave me be in pieces
Scattered around
Like ashes after the fire
No one to collect and claim.

With blatant honesty
You settle my mind
My gratitude runs deep
And I have lost my sight
Therefore, it will be a duty
For you step up and show me my place
While I put on new lenses
And see for the first time
The calamity of the hour.

Besides, if I am ever a burden
Don't hesitate to tell me,
Because I will be fine in my pieces,
Just like a phoenix burned for the ashes.

14. Phoenix

A sidewalk of thoughts
Reaching out parallelly
Can never collapse
Like a building in ruins,
It's a safe side calling
So you are cocooned,
But life is a risk, dared to be taken,
I have heard these tales
My mind is jumbled now
Searching for a muse
So I can figure my shit to put forth words again,
I am more of a reckless vagabond
Tumbling in and out of odd places
Searching for a tranquility of interphase to crumble and
merge like a horizon
So I can deem myself worthy of me
Where my reflection won't scare me anymore
And one phoenix will rise again from the ashes of
mourns.

15. Fallen Knight

A battle I fought
I won but I lost
Pride was at cost
It looked essential
It was not.

The time was right
I was leaning in the fright
I should have closed
My doors at night
As the cold seeped
With a chilling bite.

I didn't know the fight it brings
I should have left at the first ring
But I picked up phone to see the things
Tarnished hopes and frozen wings.

Unable to move, I stare at the roof
I cry and cry with broken moves
A never ending battles of turning grooves
The agony and desperation of loving you.

You were though mine but also hers
You watched me break and let me suffer
But a scratch on her you can't see
I was bleeding everywhere with wounds that seeped
You saw it all, you saved her still
My life has become like a tumbling hill
All the advices you gave it to me
You protected her always like a dying bee
Now I see I should have stopped
I can't go back and turn this clock
The future that haunts and past that mocks
I have chosen silence in this lonely walk.

How unlucky I am in this
I never had the love that I give
Too late it seems to give another try
Again this repeats like every night
So, I stopped the flight and fight
Accepting my defeat like a fallen knight.

16. It Might Take Forever

Kill me now or kill me never
What I am searching for
I found it never,
It might be too late to find my forever
It might take forever
It might take forever.

Eons passed, and time stood still,
I climbed the ecstasy and went for the kill,
A scourge whipped up of relentless will,
To find it at last
But I found it never
It might take forever
Oh! It might take forever.

Blessed is thy
With the art of favor,
Most flock to it in this dance of fervor,
I found myself savoring its newest flavor,
Then, it carved my flesh on the plates of silver,

A hefty sum I paid for this forever,
But I found it never
It might take forever
It might take forever.

17. Process

Eyes like a mirror to her soul
Reaching for him desperately
Trying to hold in some sanity
Still finding him in all the places he used to be
Realizing he is not there anymore, nor will he ever
be.

The laughter, the gazing, and getting lost in each other
It just became a fickle imagination
Ohh! But how badly she wants to move on
And not remember those times anymore
Hold herself for a moment there
And then get safely back to the shore.
As the sea is calm but still deadly, so is her heart crushed
with misery,
But she is strong, and I know that much
The bumps ahead she will overcome
Not so fast, but one by one
And then she will be standing with her head held high
An adoring smile on her face and a peaceful sigh.

18. Solace

The burden lessens, but the pain remains
I try to find solace, though, all in vain,
I tried to run, but it chased me down
Held me tight, shackled, and bound,
The frowns mar my young face
All gaze at me with such distaste,
Disdain now fills up my every core
A sheet of gloom surrounds my soul,
They glance at me with a sympathetic gaze
Trepidation looms over my blissful days,
Oh, my pity! They all say to me
See my condition and pray for me,
But a glimmer of light is all I want
To resurface again from this darkened path.

19. Monologues

I always wonder,
What if you slip through my fingers?
Like loose sand
Slipping through the cracks.

I am afraid,
What if you break?
Onto the concrete asphalt
Just like my dreams
Never to be recovered and remembered.

How much will it hurt?
If you leave
Just like if my potteries break
Which I have decorated
Over the years of hard work.

Will it be a chaos?
Or calm before the storm?
Will I surrender or become resistant?
Will you be future or lesson?

My monologues have led me nowhere
It's like an anomaly
That I can't figure out.

I hope you stay, though
I can't take more heartbreaks
While waiting for the right one
And till the right time comes along
I will have no scraps left of my fragile, boneless piece of
muscle and tissue.

It's all gore now
As I am tired of feeding life to sound romantic
I hope it won't be too late
From a dark night to daybreak
The light must shine on this dilapidated abode
Otherwise, people will admire the haunting ruins of
what could have been and will never be again.

20. Distance

Watching from a distance
I fume in the silence of doom,
My mind is in chaos
As a devil roams around
Whispering the darkest desires to me,
I burn in myself
Restraints overwhelming me
Hands twitching to hurt and bring misery
Upon someone who I crave
Seeing love in those eyes for her
Wishing those caresses on me
Full of bliss and adoration
Alas! My heart is a raging inferno,
Unable to take it
I curse and cry
Words of revenge
Dedicated to them
Without confessions,
So I sin in quiet
Still at a distance.

21. Patterns

Patterns, when get repeated
You realize it or get cheated,
How many times does it have to repeat
Until you accept your last defeat,
You give up on people, or they give up on you
This trend has become like a dirty hue
Of ugliness and amalgamation of agony
You find someone just to lose them so early,
Does it matter anymore when you lose?
When your sanity is measured in cheap dues,
They react nicely and then become the devil
You can't control this kind of evil,
You learn something
And lose some more
Only if this disease had a miracle cure,
Where people are good, they don't play
They respect the person they don't betray,
And though it won't work out
Like some nature's law
You accept the pain so red and raw,

But your mind is at peace and smiles at you
The person you met was too good to be true,
So things like this don't happen
People are born only to disappoint,
And bonds like this just never occur
You bear all losses and suffer.

22. Maa

A shrill cry, eyes searching every side
A thirsty ear longs for her lullaby,
Since birth, he has craved her touch
Just a glance at her nursing side.

That sacred tranquility he again wants
He had all those for nine straight months,
To birth him, she sacrificed her own essence
And he lost the familiarity of every sense,
Petrified, he bawls, so they hoist him into arms
To soothe the agony and tuck him calm.

He protests, always waiting for her.
To pick him up and croon the words,
A joyous rhyme of little stars
Or mockingbirds and toy cars,
But she is so bleak to the sight
Fading in distance of bright light
Among the angels wearing all white.

A halo surrounding the wild curls
A smile formed as lips unfurled,
To shower the bliss that never came
To watch over him in crisis uncertain,
Little hands hovering to touch her soul
Her bosom to touch and latch on,
But he will never find the means to it
To voice out all the needs of him,
He wishes that he can speak, so to say
Maa, where did you go away?

23. Indian Army

They were young, when they got commissioned
At an abode of glory and utter determination,
Not for namesake, but for sacrifice
A will so strong, so rare to find.

Inspired since early upbringing
They never cared much for social mingling,
Focused on target sharply
They learned to practice stealthily,
Cleared the exams with flying colors
To fly like a free bird without hindering barriers.

To stand tall in all orders
So that enemies don't dare to cross borders,
To float and set sail
To hide in bottom trails,
King of battlefields
Carrying blood and gore on the sleeves.

But behind all this glory
Lies a story
Of gratitude and selflessness
Of a lover's faithfulness
Of a mother's tear, and father's fear
Of missed festivals
Of martyrdom and survival
Of bullets and wars
Of fleshes, marred, and charred.

Just so we could be safe,
Just so no one invades,
This beautiful paradise
Our country's pride, an army of braves
Soldiers are always heroes without capes.

24. Rain O Rain

Rain O rain
Just bless on me
Just pour me down.

No traces should be left.
Of dirt, of thirst
Just wet me up, so I feel my curves.

How you move,
I want to feel in nerves
How you race,
As blood boils up.

Please sense my heat and cool it down
Touch me closer as the sunkissed dawn.

Move over me and stalk me around
Make me your prey and kiss my mounds.

Be my lover, cage my soul.
Grasp me tight, I am feeling so cold.

Just one last wish that you never stop
Keep me flooding till your every drop
Keep the circle going round and round
Rain O rain
Just bless on me
Just pour me down.

25. Lullaby

Drooping of eyes, you singing lullaby side by side
Curling of toes, stretching up to throes
Hands up in the air, arising passion so bare
Fingers that caress along the naked path of the body
Veins to trace like crooning a melody
As it goes up to down, igniting the fire that drowns
The cries of pleasure, as mouth touches lips
Smothering every bit of sound coming out
The world rips to shreds as the current reaches peak
To fall in the embrace of unfathomed bliss
Slow and sound again a new lyric begins
So I rise,
With drooping eyes, you singing lullaby side by side.

26. Euphoria

He touched me,
Starting from toes
To my knees.

He kissed me,
Two petals of my red
Then moved to the arch of my shoulder.

He devoured me,
to the mounds of heaven
Down all the way up to my horizon.

He turned me,
caressing and savoring
The elongated path of my spine
All the way to my dips.

He ravished me,
to the delicious ecstasy
So exquisite
I am left euphoric.

As I pulled him just for a final kiss
A final gaze
He surrendered till his breath escaped.

27. Knight And Maiden

He was a savage knight
She was the maiden queen
Fated to love each other
Till eternity of dimensions
In each realm, binding together.
But then there was pain, too.
Appalling and obstinate hue
Of grey paints splayed out.

A battle, a war erupted.
Vengeance was cost about life
Slow death lapsed, mourn
She died, and he bled
An oath was taken, and a prophecy was born
About the reunion of one summer born.

The lady will be all bliss.
Full of life and fairy kiss
She will heal all the wounds
With feathered touches, like a boon.

So knight traveled and stood sublime.
Visited every nook and corner of the time
And came upon his destination abode
At a meek house, bleary and old
All creaking steps and chipped soles.

He knocked and knocked and waited still
Holding his breath at the cusp of his lips
Soon, the door opened with a resounding thud
To reveal a lady like a winter dove
Pale skin and dark blue eyes
Hair as white as the beams of light.

The benevolence of love
Again struck him up
Every being was enthralled and struck
Waiting for the union
Of one knight and the maiden
A rise of a kingdom
A shine on the future
To erase the very darkness in every creature.

28. Grim Reaper

It always lurks in the shadows of bereavement
Lithe and fleet
A whirlwind of black mass
And a scythe to reap.

It is the harbinger of death.
Collecting the deceased
To the path of Styx
Fulfilling its part of the deed.

Calling out the names
Of eternal souls
Loitering around the figures
Till death is mourned.

Folklore describes its every form.
Varying from Greek to Latin
In every chrome.

With lightning speed
The death creeps
To harvest the shadows unto Hades.

With hourglass in hand
While waiting for the sand
Till the last grain is left.

Then it whips out the blade.
To take the life away
It's a timeless being
Of the realistic dreams.

An embodiment of annihilation
A silent thief
A grim reaper.

29. Harbinger

Wake up they are here,
Shadowed in the cloak
Of blackest hell
Peeking through the crevices of their pitless bottoms,
They have come to fetch
Your eternal, my dear
Into their realms.
But it's not time for you to go
Open your blinders
Earth is beautiful
We are beautiful
It's not an occasion of mourns
Of deceased funeral,
So wake up
They are here,
Loitering in seams watching,
Till you breathe your last.

30. The Last Jedi

Stardust and stargaze
This battle started to save my race,
Galaxies after galaxies
We have searched,
To come upon your place.

Many of us martyred
Over the passing years,
But as a part of the Universe's history,
You always remained shrouded in the mystery.

Nothing has touched you for so long
Darkness is what you have thrived on,
Intimidation was your cruel power
But light was always the answer,
So we searched every corner
To find that one saber,
And with blessings through the sky,
Your end came from "The Last Jedi".

31. The One That I Can't Have

I tried to stay away,
I tried to stay behind,
I tried my level best to get you out of my mind,
Just one glance at you makes me forget things
I am spinning in a circle of wishful dreams,
Mesmerized by you so easily, I get drawn
Now blurred are the lines of right and wrong,
I know it's not possible to fulfill my desire
It's just a deadly case of forlorn desire,
I have done all the science, I have done all the maths,
To see why our destiny never crosses the path
And why do I only love the one that I can't have?

32. The One Who Got Away

The one who was there but never stayed
I remember that time of the one who got away,
The one that I met with a mere coincidence
I fell in love I don't know when,
It happened too fast, and I was a fool to let go
Trusting him easily to protect my heart also,
All the nights, I remained wide awake
Still forgiving him when my sanity was at stake,
I cried, I sobbed, and I begged him that day
Yes! I do remember those times of the one who got away.

33. I Will Find You

I will find you
From the horizon of the sky
To the deepest of earth
If I have to uplift
If I have to unearth.

The mysteries you traveled
When times unraveled
Like a spiral beam
With the blackest theme
To where the moon resides
So far and bright
And the sun shines a shade darker
Full of anger and scorched laughter.

In the depths of the abyss
In spaces and pits.

But I will find you one day
Though it may be years
I will crush the dust
Of burning stars
And the cosmic cores of mass
To find you at last.

You will be scared
But worry no more
I have walked miles
In all chromes
To search for you
In faceless souls.

For it's a burning love
With an agonizing past
Shrouded in the universe
So infinite and vast.

34. I Will Love You

Under the moonlight, I will love you,
Till my last light, I will love you,
Battling your scars along with you
I will give myself in every hue.

I will take you as you are,
Thorns and petals of shapes apart,
Unlining every tattooed link
I will join it with my own ink,
But when you are unsure
I will become your every cure,
And as you love me madly
I will love you.

I will soothe your blues,
I will cover you in Dunes,
Of love and warmth,
Of lust and want,
It will be an eruption
And we will be high on smiles,

But if, at times, evil creeps
Slowly, on our love so deep,
We will stay
And chase it away,
Bruised and battered, we stand to rue
And as I promised
I will love you.

35. Waiting For You

Every time it hurts
Every time that you bleed
Every time you die slowly
For someone's greed
Just keep in mind
That there is time
Of every pain and lesson you endure
And then comes the cure.

When you see no end
You don't have to bend
Just be a little patient
And wait in the present
By letting bygones go
So that you grow.

There is wisdom in knowing
Of all the undoing
That you had to face
All that emotional wreckage

Will lead you to something
So just stop this hurting.

And even though it is tough
You are enough
To face the life
You don't need a partner in crime
And while you feel like drowning
In your surrounding
There will be a day
Where you will say
It was all for something
All the pain I have felt in
Has led me to you
I have been waiting for you.

36. You

There was nothing new
When I knew
That entering my is a guy like you.

I have met guys a few
Of which lines have blurred.
Then we started to talk
That lifted some hue
Though there is nothing new
When I knew
That entering my is a guy like you.

Days spent taking this time
I got to know why poems do rhyme
The deeper I go, the more you are
So I scratched the surface, which left the scars
Still, there was nothing new
When I knew
That entering my is a guy like you.

Now we know each other well.
It feels like casted spells.
Blissful and awake
I stare at my state
After the first date
Something feels new
That's when I knew
That entering my is a guy like you.

Ohh! It again crashed.
As expected, a new mess
It's okay, I know this one
I only know but know no one
Alas! It is nothing new
When I knew
That entering my is a guy like you

Courage is the man's armour.
I have heard, and you proved it harder
You fought strong and loved stronger
You held on to bonds with such a fervor
A firm promise of everlasting maneuver
You made me believe in the tales of forever,
Something feels incredibly new
At last, when I knew
That entering my life is a guy like you.

37. Arms Of My Beloved

Watch me fall apart
Into the arms of my beloved.
Let me shatter and break down
Onto the ground
The earth is all ours
And just like it's rawness
Let the passion flow
Onto the grassy hay.

Hair full of straws
And eyes full of stars
Gazing so deep
Where an aura of bliss is wrapped
Just like us, without an inch of space
For air to escape
But it does so very artfully
From the mouth
In short gasps
Tender touches and rough grab
All encompassed in one.

It's overwhelming on the soul
Of us benign species,
How do we handle it?
How do we escape?
The body is flowing
In the metaverse of love,
And now, time is relative
A fickle, a lightyear,
All are one.

The constellations are tempting
To join our limbs,
How do we do it?
You shall do it in sync
It's a dance of fervor
And this dancing starts
I can't help falling
So watch me fall apart.
Watch me fall apart
Into the arms of my beloved.

38. Stupid Crush

Side glances and shy smiles
Walking for you, I went miles and miles,
My eyes roam to search you off
Whispers of longing heart never stop,
My mind is filled with the thoughts of you
A battlefield erupted, but you never knew,
When my gaze connects, I skip a beat
I can feel the burn, I can feel the heat,
In the silence of the room, when I sit alone
I try to imagine the scenarios unknown,
But nothing is going to happen for sure
As one-sided attraction doesn't have any cure,
Then why does my face get adorned by blush,
When I know that it's just a stupid crush.

39. Constellations

On the coldest of winter nights
I will wrap us in a blanket tight,
Lying over the highest tower's roof
Trembling hands interlaced like a mystery,
As we will gaze into the oblivion
Questioning our very existence
On the path of Cupid's dance,
Wondering where our stars align,
Do they form a constellation?
Or they become a meteorite.

40. Atoms And Cosmos

A day without shine
In a world so blind
I met you suddenly
You felt one-of-a-kind

The pieces, when unwind
Like a beautiful rhyme
The mysteries unraveled
Like the magic of time.

I wasn't so sure
If there is more
Or the chance to be
Weaving in between
But it was the destiny
Speaking to me
What I couldn't hear before
I heard clearly.

It was bold and stark
Written in the stars
Of atoms and macros
Constellations and Cosmos.

We aligned so well
Like the witch's spell
Now the world is ours
To live and to swoon
To surround us with spring blooms
Of warmth and love
And pray to the above
That the difficulties pass by
And we survive these tides.

41. Behold

If there has to be good
It has to be you,
Surrounded by these murky blues
You felt like the sun's dusky hues,
Earthy and serene
Grounded in reality,
With a touch of mayhem
And bound with chivalry,
Of old traditions and sacraments of cultures
You are sound away from the sadistic vultures,
The laughter that shines
Erasing the eery vines,
And brings a smile
Stretching up miles,
A future untold, waiting to unfold,
Of realistic dreams and sights behold.

42. Dunes

We are two lonely souls
Staring and merging at the horizon
Morning filled with chaos
But evening painted in red hues
I love his loneliness
He adores my solitude
I share my secrets with him
He smiles and bids me adieu
He is the man of the skies
Of warmth and blues
And I am his admirer
Enchanted with his dunes.

43. Beginnings

Moonlit water and coarse sandy beach,
The sea is near but still out of reach.

I am wrapped in your arms and gazing at the shore,
My heart is beating fast as I tremble for more.

No words are needed, no need to confess,
I can feel what you feel, I can feel this mess.

Holding hands, learning every curve of it,
Turning it again so we can again observe it.

With a little bit of teasing and a voice filled with a smile,
The magic is being woven, but the bond is still fragile.

I don't know where it will lead, I don't know what it
holds,
I just want to live this moment, watching it unfold.

44. Rockabye

Rock and scissors, trees and ferns,
Got me wrapped in pinky every turn.
Nothing enchants me like a vine on the wall,
I am all beer and no wine at all.
Never one to turn into some fashion con,
The geek runs in the blood, and glasses are on.
Stumbling feet, being a klutz all the time,
Glitz and glamour, no thanks, I am fine.
Show me a corner and pile me on books,
Bribe me on food, and I am hooked.
No charm to see I am a rebel every bit,
Not made of sponge, I am a solid concrete.
But underneath here, runs passion so bare,
Emotions soar high and she just wants to fly.
Reaching all the heights, her love unwinds,
And wrapped in her cradle, she sings Rockabye.

45. Irreplaceable

This friendship that we share
Is so wild and bare
With purity of nature
And the serenity of the rain
It's thick as a lion's mane
And thin as a thread
But holds all the pride
And the pressure of the tide
The sounds of eruptions
And the melody of morning
As different as poles
But bound by strings
Of love and care
And so you are and always will be
Irreplaceable.

46. Your Essence

You might go away someday
Soon, or it may be a long way,
Never we know what the future will bring
Your spirit or body, no one can say,
But let me assure you about something
I will forever carry with me your essence.

Even though you leave me at some point
And leave me to bear every pain,
Every agonizing second that will pass
I will battle it like a warrior in war,
Face this world with a strong wall
Though I might be dying inside and all,
I won't let anyone get involved
Just you and me against this world,
I swear the days that I will live
Every breath that I will take,
I will carry with me your essence.

47. Cocoon

Let's meet, Shall we?
The shallowness of the river is calling.

The birds, when they sing,
Feel like chimes of old rings.

This place we have stumbled upon,
From this day, my heart belongs.

A peace has wrapped me up in fleece
I wonder if it's the cooling breeze,
Of the windy trails
And setting sun
Or the moon
And the magic woven and spun.

So many times, I heeded,
To come to the place I needed.

A sound mind, an even heart
Two arms felt like the start,
Of something tremendous
A gravitational pull so infectious.

I got magnetized in the wheels,
Now, time is all that I never feel.

It passes and comes another day,
Bold and quiet, I extend the stay.

To feel again the cocoon of arms,
The love that soothes me like a balm.

48. Guiding Light

A numbing presence
A sold lie,
My life was just a bold lie.

I trusted some, I lost to some,
Some beliefs cost, some faith begun.

I traveled the hills, I sailed the sea,
To search for you, to find and see.

I sought the places where you reside,
In all the glories and religions aside.

I searched the lore and scriptures of beings,
I tried to find certain truths and inklings.

My way of living was challenged to the core,
Wisdom was extinct, and knowledge was gone.

Arrested hopes and forlorn desires,
A myriad of emotions burnt in the fire.

Desperation stuck to my very essence,
I craved peace in all percipience.

I begged and howled in this pain of life,
I hit rock bottom with no shreds of pride.

Giving felt easy, so that people will mourn,
They must feel what I feel
As my life was torn.

At last! I saw you seeking me out,
It started with odd dreams and thoughts profound.

All the abandonment I felt, I feel found now,
You were always there, But I ignored the sounds.

Of your guiding light and calling to me,
I take a breath now and feel the peace.

My soul was salvaged through scads of trouble,
If the end is you, I will play this rubble.

As long as you remain as my holy grail,
Govern the passage through your incandescent trail.

49. Let Us

*Let us join our hands
But to show and not to show off,
Let us merge our voices
But to be heard and not hear,
Let us empathise together
But to feel and not fake,
Let us impart the wisdom
But to educate, not eradicate,
Let us grow with equality
But to love and not differentiate,
Let us build a world
But for peace, not destruction,
Let us laugh together
But to spread, not extinguish,
Let us create together
But to expand, not to extinct,
But let us build a legacy of love,
Of warmth and tranquility
An alternate reality.*

50. Strength

Thinking of people ranges to be different,
They will find you weak
While you gather your strengths,
You aim to reach heights
While they ponder your downfall,
But don't lock your heart
And put down a wall,
You ignite the fire to make an inferno,
And expand your wings to fly like a flamingo,
You make yourself strong and stand up tall
Wipe your tears and put on a face for all.

51. Corpse

Establishments erected
But charity lost
Darkened soul
Of blank console
A pleasant smile
Sinister thoughts,
Carrier of devotion
But love is morphed
A lifelong journey
Of naught but piled up corpse.

52. All Lives Matter

Our species is fighting battles
But not for survival,
This war is of judgments
For people who are sick and mental,
We all bleed, true
And we know the color too,
But dominance is our poison
Unfathomable and uncontrollable,
We thirst for it
So, we perform the deed,
With no penance in mind
We go truly blind,
And paint the hands red
Maybe this is how we are bred,
To hate and vengeance
With the amalgamation of mayhems,
So accurately weaved
Over the centuries
Slaving the creatures
For our personal greed,

With morons running for seats
And our voices falling on deaf,
Now, I can't see a better future
Where all lives will matter,
And equality will be given
So past sins can be forgiven.

53. One Day

One day, it won't hurt anymore
One day, you will reach the shore
One day, you will move on in life
One day, it will again alight
One day, the pain won't be there
One day, your morning will be fair
One day, you will stop this circle
One day, it won't be so hard to giggle
One day, you will start to feel anew
One day, your dreams will come true
One day, your scars will heal
One day, your mask will peel
One day, you will wonder about the future, too
One day, all the storms will be worth going through.

54. Ashes Of Our Soul

We wear our colors with all the pride
We are someone's husband, someone's wife
But still, people frown and despise
Our kind is looked upon with fright
When god graces something untold
People never fathom, never accept the unfold
Too judgemental and too blind
The world is still of a kind
To build a place, we had to chase
The bad and the good in all the ways,
Finally, it's rainbows here,
But those moments are few and rare
We have endured, and we shall do
Fight for legacy based on love
That we will build from the ashes of our soul.

55. To You, The Reader

Thank you for turning every page,
For walking with me through joy and rage
Your heart bestowed these verses a place
I am indebted in every word and way.